THE POWER OF DESIRE

OSAZEE WILLIAMS

INTERNATIONAL EDITION

Copyright © 2014 by Osazee Williams

THE POWER OF DESIRE
INTERNATIONAL EDITION
by Osazee Williams

Printed in the United States of America

Edited by Xulon Press

ISBN 9781498422475

All rights reserved solely by the author. The author guarantees all contents are original and do not infringe upon the legal rights of any other person or work. No part of this book may be reproduced in any form without the permission of the author. The views expressed in this book are not necessarily those of the publisher.

Unless otherwise indicated, Scripture quotations are taken from the King James Version (KJV) – public domain

www.xulonpress.com

Acknowledgement

To the Holy Spirit of God who is the Teacher of teachers and the Pastor over my soul, Bishop David Oyedepo; thank you so very much sirs!

And to you out there that have encouraged and helped in many several (other) ways, thank you and may your helper be near at any time you need.

Osaz.

Table of Contents

Introduction ix

Chapter 1 The Passover........................ 13

Chapter 2 Why Desire?......................... 35

Chapter 3 Even for the Wrong Reason 45

Chapter 4 How to Realize Your Desire 59

Chapter 5 What to Desire 67

Chapter 6 The Confidence We Have 75

Chapter 7 Salvation............................ 89

Introduction

"...and the Word became flesh..." "...and the Word became flesh..." "...and the word became flesh..." (John 1:14)

The above scripture kept ringing in my mind; apparently establishing the reality of life itself that we are a product of what we think and speak. My local church believes that if your heart cannot conceive it and your mouth cannot speak it, your hands cannot carry it.

A great man once said, "if you want to change your life, begin by changing your words," for the Word became flesh and dwelt amongst us as witnesses to God's commitment to His Word. Words are powerful, but yours are a function of the thoughts in your head. Words, we are told, are broken thoughts and thoughts are unbroken words. Until the word is released, the power of God to perform is helpless. Satan is also helpless without his words in your thoughts and in your mouth. Your thoughts are a function of your desires. What you desire influences what you think about. A wise man said, "your mentality shapes your reality." Even then, your mentality is a function of your desire and how you go about it.

Desire is the gateway to fulfillment and the strongest silent prayer that produces results of great effects. Psalm 145:16 says, "Thou openest thy hand and satisfiest the desire of every living thing". There are no further qualifications aside from being a "living thing" for desire to be met by the Almighty God. So your desire, no matter what it is, is obtainable in God. Although it is the desire of the righteous of which God guarantees fulfillment, we have all become the righteousness of God through Christ Jesus who knew no sin, but was made a sin offering for us who believe. In other words, as soon as you give your life to Christ, your desires become a possibility. God's greatest desire for us is that we might come to Him and to the full knowledge of His dear son, Jesus Christ, so that we may have life and have it more abundantly.

Proverbs 10:24

"The fear of the wicked, it shall come upon him: but the desire of the righteous shall be granted."

Psalm 145:19

"He will fulfill the desire of them that fear him: He also will hear their cry, and will save them."

Psalm 78:29-33

So they did eat, and were filled: for he gave them their own desire; they were not estranged from their lust. But while their meat was yet in their mouths, the wrath of God came upon them, and slew the fattest of them, and smote down the chosen men of Israel. For all these they sinned still, and believed not for His wondrous works. Therefore, their days did He consume in vanity, and their years in trouble.

For even the wrong reason, He granted men their desires. How much more will He grant the desire of a good cause and for the right reason? This is the bitter truth: truth, when told, heals. This revelation-filled book is exploring the fact that God respects your desire. I pray that the content of it brings about your total healing on every side in Jesus' name.

Chapter 1
The Passover

Exodus 12:11-14

And thus shall ye eat it; with your loins girded, your shoes on your feet, and your staff in your hand; and ye shall eat it in haste: it is the Lord's Passover. For I will pass through the land of Egypt this Night, and will smite all the first born in the Land of Egypt, both man and beast; and against all the gods of Egypt. I will execute Judgment: I am the Lord. And the blood shall be to you for a token upon the houses where ye are: and when I see the blood, I will pass over you, and the plague shall not be upon you to destroy you, when I smite the land of Egypt. And this day shall be unto you for a memorial; and ye shall keep it a feast to the Lord throughout your generations; ye shall keep it a feast by an ordinance forever.

The Passover is one of God's vital ordinances that He commanded the children of Israel to observe throughout their generation. Jesus upheld and observed this in His days. It is such an important memorial instituted by God to mark His execution of judgment upon the enemies, dictators, exactors, and taskmasters of His people, the Egyptians, and their gods. It is still potent today against anything that exact upon your flesh and life in the form of sickness, whether physical or spiritual. It was the Lord's Passover and blood that was the token of protection for His people while at the same time, the judgment and vengeance upon their enemies. The blood of the Lamb that was used as the token instrument for this mission was without blemish and a male of the first year (Exodus 12:5). Jesus was about to take the place as the Lamb in Luke 22:15 ("for He is our Passover" -1 Corinthians 5:7) and so desired to keep the ordinance alive, fitly knit it to the New Covenant in His blood that was about to unfold. It was one of Jesus' most critical periods in His earthly ministry. He had to use the force and power of desire to accomplish this dire need to sup with His disciples so that He could impact them and remind them of the victory over the enemy by the blood. Indeed the blood of Jesus is God's judgment and vengeance upon our enemies.

Luke 22:15

> "With desire I have desired to eat this Passover With you before I suffer."

Time was running out and with the thought of the agony He was about to face, He needed the force of desire to pull the Passover with His disciples.

Even Jesus had to desire to have His desire met. Desire is the fire that sets your actions aflame.

Burt Goldman said in his article on desire, belief, and expectation that events may be manipulated to solve problems you are faced with and while there is no disputing the fact that you can't always get what you want, it is also true that you can exercise your innate power over the events of your life and make things go the way you want much more frequently.

Desire is an innate power ordained and respected by God (among others) to deliver and create your world. Both poverty and riches are an offspring of your desire. Before you can get what you want, you must first desire it. You must believe it can happen and you must expect it to happen. These three forces -- desire, belief and expectation -- he said, are forces with enormous power to deliver on any issue.

Hardly anyone can live without a desire, except of course for lunatics and some other exceptions. You must desire something before you can take action that can lead to its realization. In doing this, you must believe you will have some level of gain or satisfaction from it. This distinction is important because God also has a desire concerning you that should supersede your personal cravings that may negate His purpose for your life. Like every other thing in life, desire has degrees of strength. If you examine the Syrophenician woman, who wanted healing for her child, or blind Bartimeaus, or the centurion who wanted his servant healed, and other people that constituted the multitude around Jesus at the same time, you certainly will discover that their level of desire were not all the same. Burt gave a story of a disciple who wanted enlightenment (wisdom) and his master took him to the bank of a river. The master had him kneel with his head over the water. He held the disciple's neck and pushed his head below the surface of the water. Soon the disciple began to gasp for air. After about two minutes of frantic struggle, the master released him and when he was rested, he asked him, "What was your greatest desire when your head was under the water?"

The disciple answered, "to breathe."

"Ah," the master said, "When you desire enlightenment to that degree, it shall be yours."

This is true of anything one may desire. Desire is more than mere wishing. If it is weak, it is most likely to be a wish and it is unlikely that anything will motivate you to activate your will to accomplish the object of that desire.

Let's quickly look at the desire of a king in the Old Testament and determine if this was a mere wish or a true desire and how God responded to such craving.

Isaiah 38:1-22

> In those days was Hezekiah sick unto death. And Isaiah the prophet the son of Amoz came unto him, and said unto him, Thus saith the Lord, Set thine house in order: for thou shalt die, and not live.
>
> Then Hezekiah turned his face toward the wall, and prayed unto the Lord,

And said, "Remember now, O Lord, I beseech thee, how I have walked before thee in truth and with a perfect heart, and have done that which is good in thy sight." And Hezekiah wept sore.

Then came the word of the Lord to Isaiah, saying, "Go, and say to Hezekiah, 'Thus saith the Lord, the God of David thy father, I have heard thy prayer, I have seen thy tears: behold, I will add unto thy days fifteen years.' And I will deliver thee and this city out of the hand of the king of Assyria: and I will defend this city."

And this shall be a sign unto thee from the Lord, that the Lord will do this thing that he hath spoken; "Behold, I will bring again the shadow of the degrees, which is gone down in the sun dial of Ahaz, ten degrees backward. So the sun returned ten degrees, by which degrees it was gone down."

The writing of Hezekiah king of Judah, when he had been sick, and was recovered of his sickness: "I said in the cutting off of my days, I shall go to the gates of the grave: I am deprived of the residue of my years. I said, 'I shall not see the LORD, even the LORD, in the land of the living: I shall behold man no more with the inhabitants of the world.' Mine age is departed, and is removed from me as a shepherd's tent: I have cut off like a weaver my life: he will cut me off with pining sickness: from day even to night wilt thou make an end of me. I reckoned till morning, that, as a lion, so will he break all my bones: from day even to night wilt thou make an end of me. Like a crane or a swallow, so did I chatter: I did mourn as a dove: mine eyes fail with looking upward: O Lord, I am oppressed; undertake for me. What shall I say? He hath both spoken unto me, and himself hath done it: I shall go softly all my years in the bitterness of my soul. O Lord, by these things men live, and in all these things is the life of my spirit: so wilt thou recover me, and make me to live. Behold, for peace I had great bitterness: but thou hast in love to my soul delivered it from the pit of corruption: for thou hast cast all my sins behind thy back. For the grave cannot praise thee, death cannot celebrate thee: they that go down into the pit cannot hope for thy truth. The living, the living, he shall praise thee, as I do this day: the father to the children shall make known thy truth. The Lord was ready to save me: therefore we will sing my songs to the stringed instruments all the days of our life in the house of the Lord."

For Isaiah had said, "Let them take a lump of figs, and lay it for a plaister upon the boil, and he shall recover."

Hezekiah also had said, "What is the sign that I shall go up to the house of the LORD?"

King Hezekiah's desire was to live rather than to die and be recovered of his sickness. In verse two, Hezekiah turned his face toward the wall and prayed to God. The intensity of the desire within was the driving force that made a King turn his face toward the wall. *This is the end of the road*, Hezekiah must have thought, *and my help can only come from above. The one I must cry to has what it takes and it is within His power to give and to deliver.* He did not go to any man (not even the Prophet Isaiah), for no man has the power to grant such a desire, but he ordered his cravings aright.

Verse three says, "...and Hezekiah wept sore." The heat of that desire was what forced the tears out of the King. As a matter of fact, it was not the tears that moved God, but the intensity of the desire behind the tears and the reasons for the craving. That was exactly what God granted. In fact, this desire was with clear understanding. Verse ten: "...I am deprived of the residue of my years."

Verses eighteen and nineteen: "for the grave cannot praise thee, death cannot celebrate thee: they that go down into the pit cannot hope for thy truth. The living, the living, he shall praise thee..."

The result was immediate, as Isaiah was asked to go back and reverse the pronouncement even with a sworn renowned sign in verse eight. The king knew that his years were not complete; there is a residue yet to be fulfilled. He knew God was Jehovah Rapha, the Lord that healeth us and he got everything his soul desired to be alive and well for the rest of his years. He was recovered of his sickness (verse twenty-one) and fifteen years was added to him (verse five).

Most often, one is amazed at the feat one can achieve in the face of danger, especially when life is involved. A group of young boys were playing street soccer in the neighborhood and the ball went into a high-walled compound. Desiring to continue the game, they assisted one of them with the help of a wooden ladder over the fence. Soon, the boy located the ball, but realized that the wall was too high to cross over back to his friends. So, after several attempts, those outside were devising ways to transport the ladder over the fence to him. He too began to search for something that could assist him within the compound. While he strolled toward the back of the house, a fierce looking dog that apparently was sleeping suddenly arose with a tearing bark. In a matter of seconds, the boy was outside the fence with his mates, although without the ball. The wish to live at this later time was stronger than before and therefore can be described as a desire. The result was an unusual strength and force that generated power to leap over the wall that he hitherto could not climb over after several attempts, without death being a threat.

Queen Esther knew that she could not appear before the king according to the law without his invitation, but now her people stand the risk of being destroyed. With the charge from her uncle, the force behind her craving was no longer a wish, but a desire. In Esther 4:16, she said "... and if I perish, I perish." A genuine desire will always procure for you divine favor. The scepter was not only lifted to save the life she no longer cared about because of her desire, the king was ready to grant her request up to half of the kingdom (Esther 5:3). Such is the power of desire! In the case of Hezekiah as earlier stated, his desire did not only procure him favor, but also health and length of days.

To boost your desire, take a look at -- either by imagination or by visualization -- the beneficial end result of what you desire to happen. The glory of the end result is a propelling force that will enhance your accomplishment. Jesus despised the shame for the glory that was set before him. Hezekiah saw the glory of praising God in the land of the living and celebrating His faithfulness and he went for it. The young man saw the beauty of the gift of life and with a blinding force, leaped over the wall. Esther knew she would be miserable all her life if she stayed back while her people were completely destroyed under her nostrils. All desires disappear when there is no reward or envisaged benefit. Your thoughts that can run into millions a day are bonded together by the force of desire, for it is to make meaning. Desire glues every thought to another and makes a whole of them. If desire is absent, thoughts will disappear.

The second force that Burt mentioned is belief. Whereas belief is a more general term to describe this powerful force, faith is a better and stronger term for it in Christendom. Belief is a mental acceptance, but faith is the substance of things hoped for and the evidence of things not seen (Hebrews 11:1). A great man of God, Kenneth Copeland, described faith as the heavenly substance of what you desire in your heart. This is powerful as it opens our eyes to receive, believe, and know that virtually everything needs to be desired to before it can be actualized. A good marriage has to be desired, a good job has to be desired, having and raising kids has to be desired, living a healthy and long life has to be desired, and so on and so forth. However, we do have a problem when we respect ideas or things from people we consider to be authorities and who are trusted, for example: your parents, your pastors, teachers, where they may be faulty or have a faulty foundation. You will soon discover that our acceptance still stands even when there are facts that contradict it. This confusion of course becomes a fundamental part of your thought process. When the God of Elijah came down to consume the sacrifices with fire, it altered the thought pattern of the Baal worshipers. Did they repent? No, because you only accept information or acts that reinforces your belief and reject the ones that contradict it even when the contrary is so obvious. This is one of the major reasons why it is difficult to convert people with varying upbringing and background. Of course, Jesus knowing this, said, "no man comes to my father in heaven but through me." Sometimes people say whatever you believe in works and that is true to a great extent. This is largely responsible for pagan worship in most parts of the world. Peter believed in Jesus and walked on water at His command but began to sink when he started to doubt. Peter had said earlier, "If you are the one Lord, ask me to come." Jesus did not perform any magic on him, but Peter's belief (or faith) in Jesus and His word generated the power to walk even on water.

In almost all cases, desire comes before faith. The woman with the issue of blood had a desire to be made whole. This is what took her to many physicians in the land and from whom she had suffered many things. She had equally spent all she had in order to get well, but rather grew worse. However, when her desire connected with faith, her miracle was delivered cheaply and the twelve-year plaque was destroyed and devoured. Her desire connected with faith when she heard of Jesus (Mark 5:27). Remember, faith comes by hearing and hearing by the word of God. What we hear is important, as it can either build up or destroy our faith.

Romans 10:17

> "So then faith cometh by hearing, and hearing by the word of God. "

This was not a mere wish, as she had to defile the law and press her way through the crowd to touch the holy garment. In the sight of men, her conduct was a great offense at that time and something near impossible by many and perhaps righteous fellows. This is because Moses's law in Leviticus forbids this.

Leviticus 15:25-27

> And if a woman have an issue of blood many days out of the time of her separation; all the days of the issue of her uncleanness shall be as the days of her separation: she shall be unclean. Every bed whereon she lieth all the days of her issue shall be unto her as the bed of her separation; and whatsoever she sitteth upon shall be unclean, as the uncleanness of her separation.

This was the law at the time that made the testimony unique and outstanding even to date. The force of desire will not stop at anything until it is satisfied. Once again, it procures for her protection, deliverance, and favor.

Expectation is an equal force commanding great effect in people's lives. I remember as a part-time worker in private hospital in the northern part of Nigeria, the Fulani tribe had this habit of getting healed faster when injection is administered to them, even when it is mere sterilized water. They expect their health to be restored when they take an injection and it does work like magic.

Now, when an authority you respect tells you something, the word has an effect on your physical, mental, and spiritual being. God is the final authority and when you have faith in what He says, then your expectation is most likely to be. However, with respect to your own expectation of yourself, you sometimes begin to struggle with doubts. The secret is in making yourself the authority of the things God told you. Moses delivered God's message before Pharaoh as though he was the authority himself. In fact, God told him that he had made him a god to Pharaoh and often queries why Moses had to come back to him. David spoke to

Goliath with such authority arising from his personal expectation of the contest before them. Of course his expectation was delivered. In order to ensure that everybody had access to power, God included His prophets as carriers of His authority for those who do not know Him and for those that must see before they believe. He said, "believe the Lord your God ... believe His prophets" (2 Chronicles 20:20). Your belief system and confidence level grow with more successful results, such that as you grow into a better person, and you do indeed grow better and better.

To build your expectation, start with the little things. As it is with the seed, so it is with the tree. Start with the small if you want to affect the large. It is also true that if you want to see a change in your friend, children, spouse, or parent, change your own expectation. If you begin to expect what you desire to happen, you will soon note the changes occurring. Expectation works with all people at all levels. Change your expectation and you will see the reality of your world changing to the extent you desire.

Desire can be positive or negative. It is positive when God is the reason for His glory to be seen. An example of a positive desire is when Jesus desired to eat the Passover meal with His disciples as stated earlier, and Paul the Apostle's desire to be with Christ (Philippians 1:23). Simeon's desire to see Jesus before he tasted death is a positive one. Elisha's desire to have double portion of the Elijah's anointing is a positive one. Moses's desire to suffer affliction with his people, Israel rather than savor the bounties at Pharaoh's palace is another example of positive desire.

Negative desire, however, is a form of craving, coveting, longing for, and lusting after fleshly demands. Negative desire can be fatal as fleshly desire competes with spiritual desire of the individual. They are in contest with God's worship and piety, hence God cannot be happy with them. The Bible specifically mentioned that the desire of the flesh and eye (sexual and otherwise) are not from God (1 John 2:15), but of the world and will also perish with the world. There is a caution here because lack of understanding of this area has wrecked many as they become heavenly minded (in ignorance) and earthly foolish. A few examples should suffice here:

Amnon desired his sister Tama (2 Samuel 13: 1-17) and forced her to bed. Soon after the ordeal, he hated her so much that the hatred wherewith he hated her was greater than the love wherewith he had loved her. One would wonder why the "love" that caused Amnon to grow lean and fall sick would suddenly turn to hatred of the magnitude described in the scriptures. Unregenerate persons are ruled by deceitful lusts (some call it desire) that hastily compete and contend with the spiritual desire of individual. One of its greatest characteristics is that it is hasty and of immediate gain or satisfaction and is mostly of the flesh.

The remedy is to walk in the spirit (Galatians 5:16-18) and be led by the spirit at all times. Only the presence of the Holy Spirit in the life of the believer makes victory over sinful desires possible (Romans 8:12).

Achan took of the accursed things and the anger of the Lord was kindled against the children of Israel.

Achan coveted a goodly Babylonian garment, silver, and a wedge of gold that were accursed and took them (Joshua 7:21), thus bringing severe judgment to himself and his entire family.

However, the desire to prosper, live long, and be in good health are certainly not in this category except if in doing this, you throw God's commandments to the dustbin. This is because these are what God actually wants for you. So they are in His perfect will for your life. God himself is a prosperous and prospering God. Consequently, His children must be prosperous as the seed and gene of prosperity is in them.

3 John 2

> "Beloved, I wish above all things that thou mayest prosper and be in health, even as thy soul prospereth."

Chapter 2

Why Desire?

Proverbs 13:12&19

> "Hope deferred maketh the heart sick: but when the desire cometh, it is a tree of life. The desire accomplished is sweet to the soul: but it is abomination to fools to depart from evils."

Your desire keeps your hope alive! Your desire is your gateway to your accomplishment. The Bible says that desire accomplished is sweet to the soul and that an accomplished desire is a tree of life. The major reason is because that is what God will fulfill, satisfy, or grant. God is committed to granting your good heart desires. Jesus was so emphatic when He drew an analogy in Matthew 7:7-11. A detailed study reveals the following reasons why God is committed to giving you your heart desires.

Firstly, He loves you and respects your choice. He knows that hope deferred makes the heart sick and He is our healer. The granting of the attendant desire can heal a deferred hope and that is what God does. He commanded that we should not ask another to come back again when it is in our power to do something within our immediate reach (Proverbs 3:27-28).

God is a God of covenants and will not break His covenant. This is not news. I think this is actually the problem. We are too familiar with what God says to the point that we do not respect it any longer. It has no impact or reverence anymore to people. Everybody perhaps knows that God is a God of covenants, but most people don't want to know how it works or why God should respect and hold tenaciously to operating on the covenant.

In operating the covenant of asking and receiving in Matthew 7:7-11, the covenant keys are in verses six and twelve. God will not grant the desires of dogs (verse six) neither will He give his pearl to swine. Jesus denied the syrophenician woman (Mark 7:25) her desire even when she was crying over him, because she was a "dog" and until the woman activated her faith (that is the covenant platform to obtaining from heaven), her daughter's fate remained the same. A lot of people are outside the covenant while a lot more are in the covenant, but are not walking in the covenant. The result is frustration, complaining, and murmuring that are each a great sin against God.

You will perhaps observe that God did not grant the desire of His dear Son Jesus at the cross.

Matthew 26:39 & 42:

> "...O my father, if it be possible, let this cup pass from me: nevertheless not as I will, but as thou wilt."

It appears Jesus felt that God's answer was not forthcoming. It seemed God's mind was already made up on the issue. He went to pray again and still, the situation remained the same. So he said in verse forty-two, "O my father, if this cup may not pass way from me, except I drink it, thy will be done."

How thoughtful of Jesus to recognize God's will in the matter and put His own aside for God's will to be done. The cup was a bitter agonizing one, yet God didn't wish or will it away, even after Jesus prayed because that was His part of the covenant to redeem mankind from total destruction. Yes, it was God's will, but also it is Jesus' roadmap to justification and glorification ordained before the foundations of the earth. As serious and intense those prayers appeared, they were mere wishes and do not qualify to be taken for a desire and hence God did not grant it. "… If this cup may not pass from me, except I drink it, thy will be done," does not depict someone desperately looking for something.

Often when our prayers feeling as they are "falling on deaf ears" and our praises are not procuring anything, then there is need to review God's will and purpose in the matter as well as our position with respect to whether we are merely wishing or actually desiring. Such appraisal will do us more good and it could just be a stepping-stone to the top and the higher place ordained for you.

The second covenant key is that we should do to others what we want others to do to us (verse twelve). There are certain things you will never need to pray about. They fall to you as a result of the "seeds you have sown" in the past. This is akin to the second commandment Jesus gave: to love your neighbor as you love yourself.

God wants to grant your desire because that is one sure way to advance His kingdom on the earth. Sometimes you may not even have a visible desire or have given up like the Shunamite woman (2 Kings 4:12-14) who was serving God with what she had, and God gave her what she had not. Your desire may also differ from His, like that of Jonah. God knows better. When we fulfill His desire, we often fulfill ours in a grand style.

Again, God also grants our desire for His name's sake (Isaiah 48:11). God knows the importance of desire and how they manifest in a man's life. He wants to take the glory for the manifestation of that desire. He wants full glory for whatever is good that you desire. So, God wants to grant your desire because He alone wants to take the glory. Your happiness is His priority. He is Jehovah Jireh; He is your heavenly father and you were created in His image. Many years ago, I had a desire to go to high school, but my parents weren't very "rich" and so one of my paternal uncles promised to pay my school fees. Thank God that when it was time to pay, he reneged on his promises that God alone may take the glory. I did not only go to high school, I went to college/university, and even later had an MBA and a professional certification in Public Accounting Practice. My desires were met in the face of a timid, daring situation, but God took the glory and to Him alone be all the glory forever.

God will also grant the desire of those that serve Him in order to separate them from those that serve not. There are so many ways to serve God: in tithes, offerings, services in church, well doing, with your time and your means, etc. Scripture says that the desire of the righteous shall be granted. We have all become the righteousness of God through Jesus Christ that knew no sin, but was made a sin offering for us all.

God is a prayer-answering God (Psalm 65:2); we can pray, but we cannot answer prayers. Not the Pope, not the Bishop, not a pastor, but only God answers prayers. Jabez expressed his desires in prayers, Hannah did, Elijah prayed, Paul and Silas prayed, and God granted them that which they desired. We could pray amiss when the aim is to satisfy our lust, it is only God that answers prayers and He will answer yours today because what He does for one, He does for the other, fulfilling the same condition. Desire finds fulfillment in purpose, as demonstrated in the case of Hannah and Elijah.

Finally, one other reason why God grants our desire is because He is your friend, a true friend. God called Abraham His friend (2 Chronicles 20:7, Isaiah 41:8, James 2:23). He said, "how can I do something without telling my friend, Abraham?" In other words, "how can I do something contrary to Abraham's desire?"

God's commitment to this was expressed in His "long suffering" with Abraham while contemplating the destruction of Sodom and Gomorrah. Abraham was talking with the Almighty as a man talketh with his friend and until he exhausted his desire concerning the number to save, he kept communicating. That was prayer because prayer is communication with God.

A man without desire is dead. God also has a desire; at least, He wants all men to come to repentance. He knows how it feels when a desire is not met. He is touched by the feelings of our infirmities (Hebrews 4:15).

One more important reason for a desire is that there is no prayer without a desire. Prayer is expressing your desire to or before God. It is the desire of a man that God hears in prayers, not his mere wish. There may be desire without prayer, but there are no prayers without desire. A well-organized desire produces quicker results. A well-organized desire is one that is backed by relevant scriptures and brought before God in humility. So, if you must pray, your desire must first be revealed and organized for answers to come. Even when praying in the spirit, your desire must be well rooted in your inner man and expressing same through your spirit man to God's Holy Spirit.

Chapter 3

Even For the Wrong Reasons

Dr. Napoleon Hill wrote in *The Law of Success*:

> Desire, then is the starting point of all human achievement. It has been said, and not without reason, that one may have anything one wants, within reasonable limitations, providing one wants it badly enough!

The force of desire is what produces from the storehouse of heaven: your intense heart request. Sometimes you will be amazed how and why certain desires are met. Below are instances where the reason for the desire appears to be wrong, but the force of desire delivered it to the people. This is a pointer to the fact that for the right reason, heaven will hasten the fulfillment of it. The scripture says in Psalm 145: 16 "He satisfieth the desire of every living thing." The moment it is a desire, God's hands would be tied. Have you ever wondered why God stopped Abimelech from sinning against Him while he was about to take Abraham's wife, but the same God did not stop Eve from taking the forbidden fruit even as crucial as creation was? The Bible provides the answers. In Genesis 20:6, God saw integrity in the heart of Abimelech and not desire. It was a desire, Abimelech would not have time to be dealing darling asking the man -- and later the woman -- whether they are brother and sister. The Lord confirmed that He couldn't let his integrity sin against Him.

Eve's Wrong Desire

You can contrast Abimelech's case with Eve's in the following verse:

Genesis 3:6:

> And when the woman saw that the tree was good for food, and that it was pleasant to the eyes, and a tree to be desired to make one wise, she took of the fruit therefore, and did eat, and gave also to her husband with her; and he did eat.

God saw desire and not integrity and that was all Satan needed to steal dominion from man. It is obvious that God did not travel or didn't know or was asleep or some other reason. The power of desire came into play and caused God to grant their request. This is the beginning of man's woe in the journey of life and the resultant destruction of the earth with the flood. Yet, it repented God that He had destroyed man in the flood (Genesis 8:21). Before He sent them away, He made coats for them and clothed them (Genesis 3:21). God does not want to destroy you for your want anymore and that is why this book is put together to forewarn you about how powerful your desire can make or mar you.

Cain (Gen. 4:9-15):

> And the Lord said unto Cain, "where is Abel thy brother?" And he said, "I know not: Am I my brother's keeper?"

> And he said, "what has thou done? The voice of thy brother's blood crieth unto me from the ground."

> And now art thou curse from the earth, which hath opened her mouth to receive thy brother's blood from thy hand; when thou tillest the ground, it shall not henceforth yield unto thee her

strength; a fugitive and a vagabond shalt thou be in the earth.

And Cain said unto the Lord, "my punishment is greater than I can bear. Behold, thou hast driven me out this day from the of the earth; and from thy face shall I be hid; and I shall be a fugitive and a vagabond in the earth; and it shall come to pass, that everyone that findeth me shall slay me."

And the Lord said unto him, "therefore whosoever slayeth Cain, vengeance shall be taken on him seven fold." And the Lord set a mark upon Cain, lest any finding him should kill him.

In Gen. 4:23-24, Lamech said that if God granted Cain his request after slaying his brother, Abel, willfully by avenging him seven times, then he must be avenged seventy-seven times for slaying a man mistakenly.

As stated earlier, it is not as if God did not know that Cain was going to kill his brother, but the desire in the hearts of both brothers were different. One wants to please God continually and the other is a son that wants to satisfy his master, the devil. I should think that the best place to continually satisfy and worship God is heaven and Abel desired that part knowingly or unknowingly.

For Cain too, his desire must be fulfilled and satisfied. See how he effortlessly got away with everything including a seal/mark upon him from the Lord. How humanly inequitable it seems, but the power of desire was at work and it gave Cain all he desired including first-degree murder.

Cain had a relationship with God that may not have been detailed in the Bible's account. It suffices to say that he brought an offering unto the Lord. God equally spoke with Cain and he heard Him on each occasion. A respected man of God once said that "even if God says no to you or your request, it is still good news" because at least He heard you. Cain repented of his act as confirmed by Bible scholars in interpreting Genesis 4:13 as "my iniquity is greater than it may be forgiven". Perhaps this line of thought is what gave him his heart's desire of lessening the punishment meted out by God. Verse fifteen validates the fact that God forgave him, though the consequences of his action were not removed. If Cain were slain, then God's sentence (being a vagabond and a fugitive) would have been defeated. Worst still, Cain did not walk out of his sin and sentences; he stayed with it to his own hurt all his life. It is better to fear and not sin than to sin and then begin to fear.

Thomas (John 20:24-29)

Today, every one remembers Thomas as the "doubting Thomas." Only few know and remember that he had a desire that was fulfilled as requested. Verse twenty-five: "except I shall see in His hands..." Even for the wrong reason (of doubt, disbelief and lack of faith), Jesus appeared to him to fulfill this desire. Verse twenty-seven: "then said He to Thomas, 'Reach hither thy finger and behold my hands; and reach hither thy hand and thrust it into my side; and be not faithless, but believing.'"

This strong inner request of Thomas "...except I shall see..." is absolutely contrasted with Thomas's request of John 11:16 when the disciples misunderstood Jesus to suppose that Lazarus was taking a rest by sleeping. This later occasion is more of mere wish than an inner desire of great propensity ("except I shall see...") that provoked a generational blessing upon believers in verse twenty-nine: "blessed are they that have not seen and yet have believed".

If Jesus appeared physically to a "doubting Thomas" just to fulfill his desires, how much more would He appear spiritually to fulfill your good heart's desire concerning your very area of need? Scriptures confirmed that Jesus remains the same yesterday, today and forever (Malachi 3:6).

The Israelites (Psalm 78:22-29)

Even when God was wroth with His people for disbelief and lack of trust, despite the wonders and great miracles of protection, deliverance, provisions, and so fourth, He gave them their own desire. Verse twenty-nine: "so they did eat, and were filled: for he gave them their own desire."

This was so unique: "they ... were well filled"! Not scarcely, but beyond their regular need, for they were well fed. God is able to do exceedingly abundantly above what we ask, think or imagine (Acts 2:9).

They had desired meat in the wilderness in preference to Angel's food that God provided. Again, this is an example of a wrong desire, but God granted it though with a serious cost to the people. It will remain a good prayer for a humble Christian to say, "whatever God did not give me, may I never have it."

The Seed Sower (Psalm 126:5-6)

Scriptures say that "with joy shall ye draw from the wells of salvation" and that "God loves a cheerful giver". Giving must be done willingly and cheerfully for it to be acceptable to God. Here we have two categories of people that negate this principle and covenant, yet God was provoked to give them their heart desires.

Verse five: "They that sow in tears..."

Verse six: "He that goeth forth and weeping, bearing precious seed..."

Tears and weeping are certainly not God's standard for sowing and reaping. **Joel 1:11-12:**

> Where there is no joy, the harvest perish, because all the trees of the field are withered off, but because harvest is their desire while sowing, God sets aside these laws to grant them their heart desires. ... shall doubtless come again with rejoicing, bringing his sheaves with him.

I love this translation of 2 Corinthians 9:7 from the Amplified Version of the Bible:

Let each one [give] as he has made up his own mind and purpose in his heart not reluctantly or sorrowfully or under compulsion, for God loves [i.e. He takes pleasure in prizes above other things and is unwilling to abandon or do without] a cheerful [joyous, prompt-to-do-it] giver; whose heart is in giving.

Now if they that sow in tears shall reap in joy, how much more shall they reap without fail and far beyond their expectation that sow in joy and cheerfully.

Satan and the Sons of God (Job 1:6)

I reckon that each time the sons of God came to present themselves to God, Satan also came with them (Job 1:6, 2:1). Whilst the sons of God were busy familiarizing themselves with God, Satan was busy making a demand on Him. Scripture did not record what desire the sons of men came with or perhaps they did not have any saved to appreciate

God's holiness, grandeur, and excellency. Yes, God needs these, but it does not change who He is in any form. He is more concerned with you fulfilling purpose for your life than anything else.

Satan's one strong desire was to afflict Job. So he was up and down, to and from the earth, but could not because God has sealed His blessings on Job. Therefore he came along, with the sons of men with the desire that God Himself could not resist even for the wrong reason to destroy Job and his entire family. God Himself confessed that Satan's desire moved Him against Job without a cause (Job 2:3). Satan's preoccupation as we all know, is to accuse the brethren (Zach. 3:1-4), contest, and even take it over.

When the calamities befell Job, he had no desire than to worship God. He was contented with "... the Lord gave, and the Lord hath taken away". He dedicated almost a whole chapter to curse the day he was born (Job 3:1-10). He knows how forcible right words are (Job 6:25), yet he did not use any to express his desire. He kept talking about what he had instead of what he wanted. Desires are expressed in thoughts, words, and in deeds. God will only fulfill or grant your desire and not the appraisal of your self-righteousness as Job and his friends tried to recount. If God could grant Satan's desire to destroy Job (for this is the reason because if Job had cursed God, he would have been destroyed), how much more would He grant your good heart desires, most of which are for His glory? Right and forcible words are the palm oil with which desires are presented. Twice Satan approached God to destroy Job even for the wrong reason; twice God granted his desire without the slightest hesitation. Satan took God's word back to Him (Psalm 34:7) and God could not resist His word. Whilst he also tempted Jesus, it was the same old trick he tried to employ (Matt. 4:6).

Satan's understanding of the power of desire was also manifested in Luke 22:31-32. Jesus had pray for Peter against the desire of Satan over him. You will observe that the force of that desire was strong; so much that even after Jesus had prayed for Peter, he still fell for the devil but his faith that was the object of Jesus' prayer was upheld and Peter was later converted.

Sarah Laughed (Gen. 18:11-14)

Sarah laughed for the wrong reason but Abraham had faith for his desire. Sarah laughed at the angel's declaration of her appointed time of visitation because as far as she was concerned, she and her husband were already too old and had passed child-bearing age (verse twelve). She was actually laughing at the prophesy of the angels of God rather than men's thought of impossibilities. Her laughter was not to draw from the wells of salvation but a mockery of time and those that believe God's word. If God answered her despite this, how much more will He answer those that laugh for joy at the discovery of God's word for their conditions?

Chapter 4

How To Realize Your Desire

Your desire is realizable, no matter how odd or weird. The answer to your desire is your expectation. God promised that your expectation should not be cut off (Proverbs 23:18, Jeremiah 29:11). At the end, He will give you your expectation. Desires leading to expectations from God are what provoke miracles. Daniel had expressed his desires through prayers and then was expectant. Otherwise, after three days, he would have given up or began to chase other things, but he kept his expectation alive until God sent Arch Angel Michael to dislodge the Prince of Persia. Therefore, desire expressed in prayer and backed by expectation will deliver the intended result.

One sure way to realize your desire is to address yourself and your doubt. You have to first convince yourself that you are capable of realizing your expectation from God. Unbelief is evil before God (Heb. 3:12). The father of the boy with the dumb spirit said in Mark 9:24, "Lord, I believe, help thou mine unbelief". You must believe God, you must believe yourself, and you must believe God's Prophets. Zacharias, the father of John the Baptist (Luke 1:18-20) believed God, but did not believe in himself to fulfill God's message. Verse eighteen: "for I am an old man, and my wife well stricken in years." Zacharias had a desire that he had been expressing in prayers (Luke 1:13) and now, the answer came, but he no longer had confidence in himself; he needed an explanation. This is common with most people; they have a desire, they express the same in prayers, but lose faith in themselves to actualize their expectation. Oftentimes, people fall into this when they arrogate time to the happening of events or desires. Time for marriage and time for childbearing are the worst culprits in this bracket. It reminds me of the story of the community that gathered at the public square to pray for rain, but no one had umbrella except for a little boy. Self-doubt is a major hindrance to realizing your desire. Deal with it.

Another way to realize your desired expectation is "seed" the expectation. Think about sowing a seed for a moment and the eventual harvest of the fruits of that seed. If a farmer plants a grain of wheat, his obvious desire is a good harvest. If it takes four months for the seed to grow, flower, fruit, and then mature, the farmer's expectation will increase as time elapses. In other words, the quantum of expectation will increase by the passage of time. His expectation becomes stronger in the third month than it was in the first month because he knows the timing. Each passing day takes him closer to his expectation, his desired end. The challenge most believers have is that they cannot decipher the timing of the maturity of their desires. The nation of Israel was expecting a Messiah and when He came, they did not know it and Jesus lamented that they did not know their time of visitation. Abraham did not stagger at his faith, but was strong, giving glory to God who had promised and would also do it. So, when expectations are seeded, your hope increases as time passes. It is only this kind of situation that can make the woman of Canaan to accept the status of a dog from the master's mouth without offense, but with increased expectation, joyously displaying her depth of understanding in desiring and receiving from God (Matt. 15:21-28).

Unknown to Abraham, God had set twenty-five years for Isaac to come from the day He spoke to him. If Abraham and Sarah had known this, they would have celebrated every year that passed. Who knows -- perhaps God would have shortened the time frame. So since our timing is not always God's timing, it is instructive that we continue to give thanks always in all things and at all times to Him, even as commanded by Him in 1 Thessalonians 5:18.

One sure way to seed your expectation is to identify those with the same or similar desire and begin to intercede for them in prayers. Sometimes you may even go out of your way to meet their request if within your reach and watch how God turns the situation around in your favor. It is popularly said today that Job's captivity turned when he prayed for his friends.

Closely related to the issue of self-doubt is the "practicability trap". Sarah, Zacharias, Gideon, and the officer at the gate of Samaria are few examples of people who fell for this. I am too old and past child-bearing age, I am the least, how can a measure of wheat go for so little tomorrow, when famine was such that people were already killing their children for food? It is not possible, they concluded. God's word says, "Is anything too hard for me? It may be impossible with man but not with God, for with God, nothing shall be impossible." To Mary, it was also impossible for a virgin to get pregnant without meeting any man. Though she did not drift to the practicability trap. She quickly submitted to the will of God: "be it to me according to thy word."

Again, in realizing your desire, timing is critical and crucial. No matter how relevant it is for a five year old boy who wants to marry or even drive a car, he has to wait for the right time because he is a baby at least, for the present age because anything can happen tomorrow. Most people are babies, but actually want adult stuff. You have to grow up and mature spiritually. One sure way to test your spiritual maturity is the things that still offend you about God and God's people. As you mature in the things of God, you suddenly observe that the things that gave you pleasure before are now loathed, you also begin to have more patience with the things that made you angry quickly in the past. This is a direct function of your knowledge and acceptance of God's word. Time, it is said, heals all wounds, but God's word heals faster and better.

Finally, you eternalize your desire when it is based on God's word. God's word is God's will. When Elijah desired to see Baal worshipers punished and destroyed, that was in line with God's will. So, he didn't only see the desire met, it became a reference point to date. Jesus said, "my meat is to do the work of Him that sent me." In other words, his desire is to do the work of He that sent him. This desire was met and to date is a reference point. Our desire will often greatly influence the legacy we leave behind on the earth. It starts with those little things about you: first, your family, and then your relationships, to the distant remote.

Chapter 5
What To Desire

There is something to desire; otherwise, you will desire amiss. The Scripture says that the reason why we do not have what we desire is because we ask not.

James 4:2

> "Ye lust, and have not: ye kill, and desire to have, and cannot obtain: ye fight and war, yet ye have not, because ye ask not."

Lust is another form of wishing. The above verse can be read as: "ye lust or wish, but called it desire." When you get frustrated for mistaking a wish for desire, you fight and kill because you do not know that desiring is the only form of asking that cannot be denied.

The "fear of the Lord" is the key that should be desired. It opens the floodgate to prosperity, favor, and God's mercies.

Nehemiah 1:11

> O Lord I beseech thee, let now thine ear be attentive to the prayer of thy servant, and to the prayer of thy servants, who desire to fear thy name: and prosper, I pray thee, thy servant this day, and grant him mercy in the sight of this man. For I was the King's cupbearer.

When you fear God, everything else fears you and you obtain the best of crown and the oil of joy, peace even above thy fellow. The works of God at all times is a beautiful piece to desire.

Job 14:15

> "Thou shall call and I will answer thee: thou will have a desire to the work of thy hands."

Whenever you desire what God desires, the answer is swift because God will answer speedily. Jesus said, "even if you do not believe me, believe the works that I do for they speak for themselves." Miracles and testimonies are the works of God that men should desire at all times. It gladdens God's heart and provokes Him to reproduce the same in your case. All testimonies without exception are a proof and the substance of what God desires in the matter.

The knowledge of God's ways is what brings about life and stability.

Job 21:14

> "Therefore they say unto God, 'depart from us; for we desire not the knowledge of thy ways.'"

The ways of God are the highways to a glorious destiny in all life's endeavors. David kept asking for the way to pursue or not to pursue. The way of the Lord is synonymous to direction. It is a must for everyone who desires to be great and safe.

The judgment of the Lord is sweeter than honeycomb. When the judgment of the Lord comes upon your enemies, it is sweet to your soul because you are vindicated.

Psalm 19:9- 10

> The fear of the Lord is clean, enduring forever: the judgments of the Lord are true and righteous all together. More to be desired are they than gold, yea

than much fine gold: sweeter also than honey and the honeycomb.

God's judgment is always upon the wicked. The wickedness of the wicked against God and His people are ordained for God's judgment. I have covenanted with God to cry judgment upon the wicked rather than my blood to cry vengeance like Abel or the Slain saints in the book of Revelation.

Rev.6:10-11

> And they cried with a loud voice, saying, "How long, O Lord, holy and true, dost thou not judge and avenge our blood on them that dwell on the earth?" And white ropes were given unto every one of them; and it was said unto them, that they should rest yet for a little season, until their fellow servants also and their brethren, that should be killed as they were, should be fulfilled.

When we fail to desire the judgment of God in any area, this is what happens: innocent blood crying vengeance from the ground. The blood of Jesus has been shed for us as a ransom. While still alive, you must desire God's judgment upon the wicked or your enemies by continuously crying vengeance unto the Lord. Let your spirit, soul, and mouth cry it now than to allow your blood to do so when you are dead. If Abel had cried to God for vengeance before he was slain, he would have been alive and his blood would have no need to cry from the ground.

God's house remains a refuge forever and a treasure to be desired for life. The house of the Lord is more than a mere church or a worship center. It is more of a heart connection with heaven. When you obtain God's beauty, everything about your life becomes beautiful beyond human comprehension.

Psalm 27:4

> "One thing have I desire of the Lord, that will I seek after; that I may dwell

in the house of the Lord all the days of my life, to behold the beauty of the Lord, and to inquire in His temple."

God's mercies rejoice against judgment.

Hosea 6:6

"For I desire mercy, and not sacrifice; and the knowledge of God more than burnt offerings."

We are all products of the grace and mercies of God and I am a living witness. Mercy is the opposite of judgment. While God judges the wicked, He gives mercy to the upright through Jesus, who has judged the world. Also from the verse, one other thing to desire is the knowledge of God. The more we know God, the more we excel in life, the more we enjoy life, and the more we impact lives.

Truth: the word of God is the truth and His word is wisdom.

Psalm 51:6

"Behold, thou desirest truth in the inward part: and in the hidden part thou shall make me to know wisdom."

Psalm 37:4

"Delight thy self also in the Lord; and he shall give thee the desire of thine heart."

To desire the truth is to desire God's word and to desire God's word is to desire wisdom and wisdom is the principal thing. It answers in all spheres of life except when it is corrupted.

Chapter 6

The Confidence We Have

1 John 5:14-15

> And this is the confidence that we have in him, that if we ask any thing according to his will, he heareth us: and if we know that he hear us, whatsoever we ask, we know that we have the petitions that we desire of him.

If we take a closer look at these verses of scripture, certain important words or phrases are key: First, "confidence". It means assurance, certainty, and much more in this contest, it means secret. This is the secret of men who turned to God in prayers knowing His will or asking for His will in the matter as they approach the throne of grace. If you know God's will concerning any issue (such "will" are replete in His word), your confidence that He will answer you is apt and that fuels your desire and expectation. Therefore confidence comes more as a result of what we know and believed.

Second, "anything". This means "anything"; not some things or a few things or even many things; anything is everything. If God meant otherwise, He would have said so. Anything from spiritual to physical, from health to wealth, from far to near, business, economy, career, are all-inclusive.

Third, "according to his will". This qualifies the "anything", unless it is according to His will, we often labor where the harvest is past and our desire bestow shame, reproach, and disappointment.

Fourth, "he heareth us". Hearing does not equal to answering. Jesus heard the Canaanite woman (Matt. 15:22-23), yet He wouldn't answer her. When He eventually answered her, He did not grant her request or desire until she activated her faith. In other words, until her asking came in line with God's will, she was ignored. Faith is what unlocks heaven's gate to us so that we could go in and collect our desire.

Finally, we know we have the petitions we desire of Him. Our asking must never be in doubt or wavering as James puts it, otherwise the asking will be in vain.

Hannah in 1 Samuel 1:9-19

> So Hannah rose up after they had eaten in Shiloh, and after they had drunk, now Eli the priest sat upon a seat by a post of the temple of the Lord. And she was in bitterness of soul, and prayed unto the Lord, and wept sore. And she vowed a vow, and said, "O Lord of host, if thou will indeed look on the affliction of thine handmaid, and remember me, and not forget thine handmaid, but will give unto thine handmaid a man child, then I will give

him unto the Lord all the days of his life, and there shall no razor come upon his head." And it came to pass, as she continued praying before the Lord, that Eli marked her mouth. Now Hannah, she spoke in her heart; only her lips moved, but her voice was not heard: therefore, Eli thought she had been drunken. And Eli said unto her, "How long wilt thou be drunken? Put away thy wine from thee." And Hannah answered and said, "No, my Lord, I am a woman of sorrowful spirit: I have drunken neither wine nor strong drink, but have poured out my soul before the Lord. Count not thine handmaid for a daughter of belial: for out the the abundance of my complaint and grief have I spoken hitherto." Then Eli answered and said, "Go in peace: and the God of Israel grant thee thy petition that thou hast asked of him." And she said, "let thine handmaid find grace in thy sight."

> So the woman went her way, and did eat, and her countenance was no more sad. And they rose up in the morning early, and worshipped before the Lord, and returned, and came to their house to Ramah: and Elkanah knew his wife; and the Lord remembered her.

Hannah's greatest desire was that God should look upon her affliction and remember her. The affliction was the mocking of men in respect of her childlessness. She knew that if God remembers His covenant of mercy and fruitfulness, her case shall be settled. She had been coming to Shiloh with her husband wishing rather than desiring the fruit of the womb. In this particular Shiloh however, she reversed the order; in the bitterness of her soul, she prayed, wept sore, and made a vow. These are all evidences of a desiring soul, not a mere wish. Further, the desire to activate God's covenant and her willingness to surrender the product, the fruit thereof, provoked her miracle, Samuel. There were many who went to Shiloh that year, perhaps with various desires including social activities, but she knew what she wanted; her heart connected heaven and God's willing hands were released in her favor. She demonstrated that her desire was not for her glory, but for God's when she covenanted to give the son back to God's service all his life. God knew that she meant it from her inner heart and would do it. In Hannah's time, a vow is an extreme case of desperation to obtain one's desire. It was respected and honored by men of understanding for it is better not to make a vow than to make one and not fulfill it. At the end, God fulfilled His promises and Hannah kept hers, too.

In contrast, James' mother desired something for her children too, that one of the children should sit at the right hand of Christ and the other at His left when He ascends His throne. God turned down this request because it was for selfish reasons and obviously not in His will as such. Every parent wants their children to be greater than they are. This is not out of place, because even God wants the same thing for us. However, whatever desire we have that is put back in God's hands, multiplies back to us, and certainly takes precedence over every other in God's Kingdom.

Hezekiah in Isaiah 38:1-8

Whereas Hannah wanted God to remember her based on His covenant, Hezekiah desired that God remembered his own good works, his walk in truth, and with a perfect heart (verse three). A person's good work is a covenant point of contact to elicit heaven's response to your desires. This can be a "good deed" to God's people as in Nehemiah 5:19 or for God's house or project as in Nehemiah 13:14. We cannot forget the covenant of seedtime and harvest: "whatsoever a man sows, that shall he reap."

Blind Bartimeaus

Blind Bartmeaus provoked answers to his desire by calling God's name continuously until he was heard. The cry was from his inner being, a cry of faith that heaven could not just ignore. He despised men's voice of reasoning and pulled heaven's attention over his desire, and victory was recorded. I pray that today would be your own day of victory over that issue in Jesus' name! Jesus was passing by the way of Bartimeaus as He is constantly passing by our own way on a daily basis (in churches, seminars and outreaches, prayer meetings, on televisions and radios, in books such as this one you are reading, etc.). God knows your situations and challenges and would therefore attend to your needs as He deems fit.

This event opened us to the reality of the power of desire. God needed him to declare his desire, even though He knew he is blind. Quite often, we call upon God but without a desire and some other times for offence, as was the case of John the Baptist who sent his disciple to Jesus for offence. He must have reasoned in his mind that if Jesus was truly the one that is to come, He should have seen him in prison and then come to rescue him. Offence, murmuring, and bitterness destroy desires that would have otherwise drawn heaven's attention to the situation.

Solomon in 1 Kings 3:13

"And I have also given thee that which thou hast not asked, both riches, and honor: so that there shall not be any among the Kings like unto thee all thy days."

It was not Solomon's great love for God that brought about his turnaround and establishment to bear. It was his desire (2 Chron. 1:10-12) to have wisdom and knowledge to judge God's people that earned him a place in eternity. God was particularly impressed that Solomon's desire was not for selfish interests like riches, long life, or the head of his enemies (that surrounded him at the time). Solomon's heart desire was not known until his encounter with God and as soon as God realized that this desire was in His will, He gave much more than Solomon could ever ask. God wants to bless us with all spiritual and material blessings, but it must be according to the rules so as to establish His righteousness continually. God is saying today as of old, "ask what

I shall give thee". May your response gladden His heart as that of Solomon.

Solomon appears to have prioritized his desires, but he put God's Kingdom first: "how to govern this thy so great a people." This desire activated the covenant principle of "seek ye first the Kingdom of God and his righteousness and all these things which the Gentiles seek shall be added to you". Note that Solomon's love for God brought God Himself to him. God does go to people with certain qualities and virtues in the Kingdom – love, faith, meekness, integrity, hope, etc. At other times, men have to go to God like Jabez did to obtain his desires. His desire was made through his prayers (1 Chron. 4:9-10). He honored God; for the Bible says, "I will honor him that honors me." Jabez was an honorable man of the genealogy of Caleb. His prayer request was demanded honorably and God honored him by granting his request. A recap of that prayer in verse ten is indeed an honorable one.

> And Jabez called on the God Isreal, saying, "Oh that thou would bless me

indeed, and enlarge my coast and that thy hand might be with me, and that thou wouldest keep me from evil, that it may not grieve me!"

Elisha in 2 Kings 2:1-14

Elisha had a desire that his powerful master, Elijah, described as "a hard thing". Certain desires are actually hard things and sometimes appear impossible in the hearts of men, but not with God; for with God, nothing shall be impossible. Elisha's near-impossible desire had two important attributes that should be emulated.

First, he was focused. He didn't allow anything to come between him and his desire. His response to the sons of the prophets was "I know it hold your peace". His response to his urging master, who tried to discourage him from following, was "as long as the Lord liveth and as long as..." and then, when Elijah told him it was "a hard thing", he was not discouraged.

Second, his request was to God and his expectation was from God and not even his master. He was a faithful follower of Elijah, his master, but his faithfulness was unto the Lord, not unto man. Consequently too, the rewards of faithfulness are from God and not from man. After he took the mantle that fell from Elijah, it was Elijah's God that he called out to by the riverbank and his first miracle of authority was established.

Simon the Pharisee in Luke 7:36-47

One of the Pharisees also desired that Jesus eat with him at his house. If you understand the relationship between Jesus and the Pharisees, this is possibly a request that would have been turned down. His desire compelled Jesus, who knowing all things, saw afar off another desire of a woman in the city for salvation. Most desires are quickly attended to when God sees a connection to desires in a bigger picture. The genuine desire for salvation and the desire by faith are two strong keys that often deliver instantaneously. It is clear in verse forty-seven that no matter your situation, God will not turn down any request in these regards. As a matter of fact, this is the starting point for everyone and for anyone. A genuine repentance and a heart of faith are righteousness before God and will continue to procure a man's heart desire in His Kingdom.

Chapter 7

Salvation

Jesus told us a number of parables concerning the Kingdom of God. Amongst them is the parable of the Prodigal son.

Luke 15:11-32

> And he said, "A certain man has two sons: And the younger of them said to his father, 'Father, give me the portion of goods that falleth to me.'" And he divided unto them his living. And not many days after the younger son gathered all together, and took his

journey into a far country, and there wasted his substance with riotous living. And when he had spent all, there arose a mighty famine in the land; and he began to be in want. And he went and joined himself to a citizen of that country; and he sent him into his fields to feed his swine. And he would fain have filled his belly with the husks that the swine did eat: and no man gave unto him. And when he came to himself, he said, "How many hired servants of my father's have bread enough to spare, and I perish with hunger! I will arise and go to my father, and I will say unto him, 'Father, I have sinned against heaven, and before thee, and am no more worthy to be called thy son: make me as one of thy hired servants.'" And he arose, and came to his father. But when he was yet a great way off, his father saw him, and had compassion, and ran, and fell on his neck, and kissed him. And his son said unto him, "Father, I have sinned against heaven, and in thy sight, and am no more worthy to be called thy son." But the father said to his servants, "Bring forth the best robe, and put it on him; and put a ring on his hand, and shoes on his feet: and bring hither the fatted calf, and kill it; and let us eat, and be merry: for this my son was dead, and is alive again; he was lost, and is found." And they began to be merry. Now his elder son was in the field: and as he came and drew nigh to the house, he heard music and dancing. And he called one of the servants, and asked what these things meant. And he said unto him, "Thy brother is come; and thy father hath killed the fatted calf, because he hath received him safe and sound." And he was angry, and would not go in: therefore came his father out, and entreated him. And he answered and said unto his father, "Lo, these many years do I serve thee, neither transgressed I at any time thy commandment: and yet thou never gavest me a kid, that I might make merry with my friends." But as soon as thy son was come, which hath devoured thy living with harlots, thou hast killed for him the fatted calf. And he said unto him, "son, thou art ever with me, and all that I have is thine. It was meet that we should make merry, and be glad: for thy brother was dead, and is alive again; and was lost, and is found."

Salvation is to be desired and not merely to be wished. This is one of the reasons why we have many casualties in the body of Christ today.

Salvation is more than mere confession. It is an inner craving for the translation from the rule and dominance of the power of darkness to the rule and power of light, from the kingdom of Satan to the kingdom of God. It is a spiritual tussle that is much more than what you see on the physical.

When Jesus told the parable of the prodigal son, He illustrated two major kingdom principles that may be mysteries on their own. First, the compassion of God (verse twenty) and mercies are unsearchable and rich toward all. Second, and more importantly, is your desire that God cannot just wish away, much less deny, you of. The prodigal son initially demanded of his father what is not rational or responsible at the time (verse twelve). Next, he demanded after a well-thought and carefully organized desire, to be reinstated (verses seventeen through nineteen). The condition in which he found himself was not one to be wished away, but required a strong desire for a change. He desired to be reinstated even as one of the hired servants. His father saw his desire and not his mere confession or wishes. No matter how far you have gone on a wrong road or journey, it is never too late to turn back. His desire procured for him much more than he had bargained for.

You can contrast this with his senior brother who owned everything their father had, but had no desire. He "lacked" in the midst of plenty because he never asked and the reason he didn't ask is because he had no desire. Desire contains the asking, seeking, and knocking of Matthew 7:7-8. You will observe that the "ask, seek, and knock" in these passages are not the mere wishing as some people think. It has to be deeper and stronger to merit answers from heaven. Until then, it is not a desire and cannot secure your request.

Lust can shipwreck you as we saw in the case of Judas Iscariot and Absalom. Whilst Judas lusted after money in betraying his master, Jesus, Absalom lusted after power and authority. Unfortunately, the desire of their intended victims prevailed because they didn't have a desire, but lust.

The power of desire works for all people of all ages, of all nations and for all things. If it is a desire, it will be delivered. There was a man who desired to see the consolation and salvation of Israel before he tasted death and God granted his request.

Luke 2: 25-32

And behold, there was a man in Jerusalem, whose name was Simeon; and the same man was just and devout, waiting for the consolation of Isreal: and the Holy Ghost was upon him. And it was revealed unto him by the Holy Ghost, that he should not see death before he had seen the Lord's Christ. And he came by the Spirit into the temple; and when the parents brought in the child Jesus, to do for him after the custom of the law. Then took he him up his arms, and blessed God, and said, "Lord, now lettest thou thy servant depart in peace, according to thy word: for mine eyes have seen thy salvation, which thou hast prepared before the face of all people; a light to lighten the gentiles, and the glory of thy people Israel."

Simeon did not only desire to see, but also, was expecting the salvation of his people, Israel. The salvation and consolation of Israel was a big deal at that time and it was worth waiting for because many great prophets had desired to see this period, but did not. The gracious promise made to Simeon was born out of his desire to see God's salvation and consolation of Israel. This had to happen before he died and so, the Spirit directed him to go to the temple at that moment, to see what he had long desired to see. Thus "the same Spirit that have provided for the support of his hope, now provided for the transport of his joy". At this point, Simeon did not only see Christ but also had Him in his arms. What a blessed man he was, to see his desire offered much more than he initially required or expected (1 Corinthians: 2-10). Desire will always ventilate greater possibilities when it is above the love of life and the fear of death. Simeon's pleasant desire concerning himself was far above this: "Lord, now lettest thou thy servant depart in peace, according to thy word: for my eyes have seen thy salvation."

Matthew Henry wrote concerning this: "The eye is not satisfied with seeing (Eccl. 1:8), until it hath seen Christ, and then it is. What a poor thing doth this world look, to one that hath Christ in his arms and salvation in his eyes!" Similarly, your ears will not be satisfied until you have heard and received the word of God.

Ecclesiastes 1:8

> "All things are full of labor; man cannot utter it: the eye is not satisfied with seeing, nor the ear filled with hearing."

Simeon has heard God's word and promises; his eyes have also seen Christ. His desire was matched with faith and expectation, so he could look death in the face without the terror of it, but with a sense of welcoming gain and accomplishment. It does not matter at what time you meet with Christ, whether before, during, or after falling, the effect is the same to give you life, more abundantly, before and after physical death. Scriptures say that death is the last enemy to be destroyed and the coming, ministry, death, and resurrection of Jesus Christ did finally destroy death. This is why any life without Christ is full of crises. So if you have not yet given your life to Christ or have, but stepped aside or you are not sure of any, I would like to invite you today to meet with the owner of the universe, Jesus, by simply saying or praying the following:

> *Lord Jesus, I come to you today, a sinner. Forgive me for all my sins and wash me clean by your precious blood. I know and believe you died for me and rose again for my justification. I accept you today as my Lord and personal Savior. Come and take your place in my life and write my name in the book of life. Send your Holy Ghost to me and give me grace not to look back to my vomit. Thank you Lord for now I know I am born again.*

Congratulations! Please locate a living church and continue to enjoy God's presence forever more.

If you are already born-again, what an awesome privilege. You just need to tell someone else the liberty, joy, peace that abounds in Christ. You are blessed!

About The Author

Osazee Williams (aka Osaz) is a Chartered Accountant and a Tax Practitioner. He is also an American certified Aircraft Dispatcher having undergone the training and passed the required examination for the issuance of the license. He has also undergone training in Financial Journalism. However, he asserts that his greatest qualification is BA (Born-Again). Having given his life to Christ in 1977 under the then Scripture Union (S.U.) during his early secondary education, his walk with God has constantly progressed through thick and thin. He is a wisdom merchant having also strong bargaining skills. He is married with children.

www.ingramcontent.com/pod-product-compliance
Ingram Content Group UK Ltd.
Pitfield, Milton Keynes, MK11 3LW, UK
UKHW022215230426
12048UKWH00016BA/869